FELLWANDERER

FELLWANDERER

The story behind the Guidebooks

BY

A Wainwright

1966

**WESTMORLAND
GAZETTE
KENDAL**

Printed by
TITUS WILSON & SON
KENDAL
ENGLAND

To FELLWALKERS
PAST, PRESENT AND FUTURE

PICTORIAL GUIDES
TO THE LAKELAND FELLS

a.wainwright

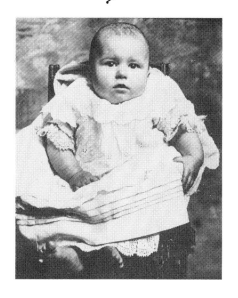

Once upon a time

and some time later

Pikes Crag, Scafell Pike

Summit of Sergeant Man, looking to Helvellyn and Fairfield

Summit of Pike o' Stickle, looking to Harrison Stickle

The Whiteside ridge, from Hopegill Head

Summit of Froswick, looking to Thornthwaite Crag

Grasmoor and Crummock Water

Robinson and Newlands Pass

Scafell Pike and Ill Crag, from Throstle Garth

Langdale Pikes, from Lingmoor Fell

The Troutbeck Valley and Windermere

Crummock Water and Loweswater, from Lad Hows

Blencathra, from Mousthwaite Col

Long Side and Ullock Pike

Robinson, from Scope End

The Buttermere Valley

Summit of Coniston Old Man, looking to the Scafells

Summit of Pillar, looking to the Scafells

Summit of Helm Crag, Grasmere

Fairfield and Seat Sandal, from Steel Fell

Summit of Broom Fell, looking to Lord's Seat

Summit of Gavel Fell, looking to High Stile

Skiddaw and the Vale of Keswick, from Catbells

Blea Crag, High Spy, looking to Helvellyn

Skiddaw, from Derwentwater

Summit of Red Pike, Buttermere

This is a book of random thoughts and recollections. It is intended, in essence, as a short and slight discursion on fellwalking; short because fellwalking is something to do rather than talk about, and slight because the subject is not a serious one. Fellwalking is action, and fellwalking is fun. You have only to sit by the Rossett Gill path to witness the action and appreciate the humour. In places I shall digress from the theme, no doubt, for I have always been easily tempted from the beaten track, and I must rely on a proved sense of direction to lead my steps back to the trail I am following. And in part, in small part, the book will be autobiographical, but not more than is necessary to link together in a chain several personal events that seemed unrelated at the time, and yet, looking back, can be seen as milestones along the same road. I promise to be brief with these details. Writing in the first person is best reserved for private letters. Here it will be unavoidable to some extent, the reason being that a correspondent (a single one, not ten thousand) recently suggested that I should write "the story behind the guidebooks" and as I had waited a long time for somebody to suggest just that, I blessed him and told him I would. This book is the result. It would be an easier commission, and make better reading, if I had some thrilling adventures to recount, some hair-raising exploits to recall. But I haven't. I have found the fells placid, and they have made me placid and given me a wonderfully serene pleasure, always.

Inevitably, what I have to say will have, must have, the Lakeland fells as a background. They cannot be other than a background to my writing for they are the background to my life. Especially that part of them above the intake walls. The rough fell country above the limits of cultivation has, through long acquaintance, become my special delight, my pet obsession. I have walked in a happy but observant trance all over it. There are many people—shepherds, farmers, huntsmen and followers, rain-gauge readers and surveyors—who know their own particular areas much more intimately, but probably few who have roamed the whole district so extensively and with the sole object of seeing what there is to be seen: not the obvious things only but those also that are hidden and those that are nearly forgotten. I have followed all the usual paths many times, until familiar with every boulder (especially those that can be comfortably sat upon), every streamlet, every bog and every rash of stones along the way, but I have preferred most the secret places that must be searched for, the drove roads and neglected packhorse trails, the ruins of abandoned industries, the adits and levels and shafts of the old mines and quarries, the wild gullies and ravines that rarely see a two-legged visitor. The beauty of the Lake District is there for all to see. The glory of the mountains is there for all to see who climb. The secrets are for those who wander from the trodden ways.

Windermere

My weekend wanderings in these silent and lonely places, far removed from the other world that pulsated in five-day spasms starting every Monday, gradually developed within me a close knowledge of the geography of this delectable corner of the country and an increasing attunement to the unique and indefinable atmosphere of Lakeland that adds so subtle a charm to so obvious a beauty. I found this the life enjoyable, up here on the quiet summits, not down there in the crowded streets. Up here, one stands back from a too-familiar environment like a painter before his canvas and views events in true perspective. Friday's worries are seen to be nothing, after all. The only things that matter are immediate: the next foothold, the drifting mist, the darkening sky. Life is challenging, and, stripped of its pretences, life is good. With climbing comes an uplift, not only of the body but of the spirit and the mind. There is no competition here with one's fellows, no silly jealousies of the man in the next salary grade; one's aspirations are simple and decent. There is no worshipping of false idols on the mountains, but, instead, deep awareness of a Creator.

The correspondent who suggested that I should write "the story behind the guidebooks" meant, of course, as if you didn't know, the seven pictorial guides I compiled for my own pleasure in the years 1952 to 1965, both years inclusive as the buff forms say. There isn't really any story—but wait a minute, perhaps the buff forms did have something to do with it. I got so many at the office—circulars, questionnaires, notifications, directions—and not one was welcome. Buff forms never are. But on Sty Head there weren't any. I could never really tolerate the language of officialdom and bureaucracy. But the talk of the shepherds fascinated me. Red tape gave me the willies. But the informalities of the Corridor Route evaporated them. Besides, a new era was dawning, even in stuffy local government offices. Machines were coming in and their coming made uncomfortable the men who had been taught to work with their hands and think with their brains. Accountancy was my line. I was a pen-and-ink man. I was trained to believe that accountancy is an art, and it seemed to my juvenile reasoning in those far-off days that accountants must therefore be artists. I remember being told that every page of my ledgers should be fit for framing. I never saw anything that came out of a machine that was. Machines are monsters and they produce little horrors.

Yes, perhaps the idea of the books generated first and foremost as a line of escape.   Some people escape in dreams but I was fortunate enough to live in a perfect dreamland that actually existed.   I was always happier pulling on my boots in a morning than putting on my shoes.   On a day when I didn't have to wear a collar and tie I was a boy again.   If I was heading for the hills, and not the office, I could set forth singing, not audibly, heaven forbid; just in my heart.   I was off to where the sheep were real, not human.

Greenhow End. Fairfield

I was not born to the good fortune of a life in the Lake District.   My childhood, boyhood and youth were spent in Blackburn, in an environment of dingy houses and shabby streets, of gaunt mill chimneys and huge factory walls that shut out the sun, of flickering gaslamps, hot-potato carts, fish and chip shops, public houses. The weekly excitement was the "penny rush", the Saturday matinee at a cinema usually referred to, rather unkindly but not without justification, as the flea-pit; later in adolescence it was the football match at Ewood Park.   There was little else to look forward to.   One does not dream much when spending-money is a penny a week.   Sunday was different, but not inspiring.   Unemployment and poverty savaged the decency of people, made the young old too quickly.   But I was not unhappy, and not different from my playmates.   None of us ever had two pennies to rattle together but there were always tin cans to kick around, caterpillars to keep in matchboxes, cigarette cards to collect; and outside the town there were fields and low hills.   I was twenty-three before I could afford a holiday away from home.   I had heard of the wonders of the Lake District.   It was only sixty miles away, but, until now, another world, distant, unattainable.   I went there with a cousin for a week's walking. I was used to walking; you had to walk in those days if you wanted to go anywhere and hadn't the tram fare. Well, I was utterly enslaved by all I saw.   I gazed in disbelief at the loveliness around me.   I had **never thought** there could be beauty like this, never imagined such enchantment, never known there could be so much **colour** and charm in a landscape.   Here were no huge factories, but mountains; no stagnant canals, but sparkling, crystal-clear rivers; no cinder paths, but beckoning tracks that climbed through bracken and heather to the silent fastnesses of the hills.   Here was quietness, not noise.   Here were flowers, not weeds.   And we were free to wander: that was the special joy of it.   We could stand and admire the heights from the valley, or we could climb and be part of the scene.   We could look at the mountains from the lakes, or we could look at the lakes from the mountains.   There was a new and wonderful freedom here: it wasn't necessary to wait until the policeman had passed on his beat.   And there was carefree exhilaration, and beauty that brought tears.   The people of the villages and valleys were friendly and kind, as indeed were the people of Blackburn, but here they had a tranquillity of character, a shy and quiet contentment I had not experienced before but could understand.   Everything was wonderful, even the rain.   That week changed my life; its haunting perfection gave me no rest afterwards.   For me there could be no other

Dove Crag, Dovedale

place, and when in due course an opportunity offered itself the Lake District became my home. Truly my home. Not merely a place to work and eat and go to bed. A place to live. A place to be. I had no roots there, but I resolved to grow some, and they would go deep, into the very rocks.

Even then, only the weekends could be spent on the hills, and they were not enough. Unavoidable evening meetings took up much leisure time: all the more reason why I should value the hours that were my own. The Ordnance map and Baddeley I knew by heart. Something else was needed. I started to draw pictures. Not of people, or buildings, or street scenes, not of aeroplanes and trains and things. Of mountains. It was fun at first, then a fascinating pastime, building a mountain on a blank sheet of paper. Let's do Great Gable as seen from Lingmell, say, in ink, with a pen: what memories it invokes! Gradually is fashioned the domed summit, where you have so often relaxed and watched clouds sailing overhead after the labour of the climb; Westmorland Crags, where you once met an old professor who told you how the mountains were formed; the rocky tower of White Napes, this reminding you that you have never yet actually visited the cairn there; the Napes Ridges, a shadowed scar on the breast of the mountain; the South Traverse, where you met that girl you would have liked to see again, but never did; the Sty Head track coming up from Wasdale Head that you have trodden scores of times; the Breast Route where you once experienced a snowstorm in May. Memories crowd in on you as you delicately bring to life on paper the various features of the mountain you have seen so often. Your pen moves through a mist of dreams . . . Yes, drawing was a good idea. It brought the mountains to my own fireside. I could wander over them seated in an easy chair, on a black winter's night, too. Mind you, the way I did it was cheating. Not for me the patient wait on a fellside boulder for the right conditions, the day-long vigil on the same tuft of grass while the details were faithfully transferred from sight to paper; not for me the carrying up of easel and equipment. Life was too short, too rushed, and, besides, it took enough effort to get myself up on the hills without further burdening myself with impedimenta. To see me climbing the last hundred feet on Bowfell, you'd think I was at 25,000 feet on Everest. No, a momentary halt and a clear photograph were enough for me. I was a cheapjack at the game. But I am sure fidelity to the scene has not suffered. A photograph captures the picture as it is seen in an instant of time, whereas a drawing done on the spot takes hours, during which the shadows change shape and position as the sun crosses the sky; and the result, because the human eye cannot register all the detail or comprehend the relationship of a single detail to the whole, even in a thousand quick glances, is likely to be not less accurate. It is necessary only to remember that the ordinary camera lens tends to depress verticals and extend distances, and correct these imperfections. But the detail, and the relationship of one feature to all the rest, is foolproof. I wasn't aiming to be an artist, anyway. My aim was to draw

The Vale of St. John's

mountains, not in a romantic and imaginative sense, but as they are.   Yes, I was a fraud.   With me it was the result that mattered, not the means.

An important happening as far as I was concerned, but which passed almost without comment at the time, was the publication by the Ordnance Survey, for general use, of maps of the Lake District on a scale of $2\frac{1}{2}$ inches to the mile.   These were grand.   They fascinated me.   The one-inch maps we had had to be content with before suffered from an absence of detail: they were magnificent maps, magnificently drawn and magnificently accurate, but on the rough country of Lakeland, where summits and crags and tarns and streams were bewilderingly crowded in small compass and where the ground was so steeply sculptured that the contours almost touched, there was simply not room on the one-inch maps to show every feature that a walker would encounter on his travels.   And the missing details are important.   If a man is trying to get on the top of Scafell from Mickledore, it is no help to carry a map that shows the location of Helvellyn in relation to Ullswater: what he needs is a map that shows him in detail how to get on the top of Scafell from Mickledore, and this the one-inch map could not do and it was no fault of the cartographer: there was no room.   But the $2\frac{1}{2}$-inch scale was release from a strait-jacket.   It gave more breathing space: it permitted the inclusion of more detail, and particularly important detail in the form of walls and fences, which are often the only identifiable and reliable landmarks on the fells in bad weather.   Mist in the valleys doesn't matter; on the hills it does and there is nothing more reassuring than to come across a stone wall and have a map that will pinpoint your position and show precisely where the wall will lead if followed.   There is no guide more reliable than a stone wall.   The $2\frac{1}{2}$-inch maps quickened my interest in the detail of the fells, and it was a thirst for this knowledge that led me in due course to use the Ordnance maps on a scale of 6 inches to the mile, which provided still greater detail, such as sheepfolds, boundary posts and mine levels.   And, because the 6-inch maps had not been completely revised for a great many years, and were thus in this respect out of date. they presented a fascinating picture of Lakeland as it was around the turn of the century and indicated the roads and paths engineered to serve the mines and quarries and sheepfolds since abandoned.   It became a joy to me to trace these old ways by which now-forgotten men had journeyed to and from now-forgotten places of employment.   The 6-inch maps quickened my interest, and stimulated my imagination, in industrial Lakeland.   It is hard to believe, as we nowadays walk many of the more desolate daleheads and fellsides, where sheep graze undisturbed, that they were once a scene of human activity.   Only the ruins of industrial enterprise remain today.   Silence is always more profound in places where once there was noise.   More people than ever are walking the hills, but there was a time, not long ago, when they carried a greater population: not men out for pleasure but men slaving for a living in conditions that now seem appalling. They were the tough men, not the present visitors who today 'do' ten summits a day.   Those men had no eye for the summits.   Nor time.   Nor inclination.   There was work to be done, hard work.   Nobody demanded of them a $3\frac{1}{2}\%$ increase in productivity each year.   They were on maximum effort from the start.   They had to be.

Kirkstile, Loweswater

But I was writing about maps.   An inspiring feature of the larger-scale maps is that they give the illusion that one is covering more ground more quickly.   Using the one-inch map a walker may spend all day frigging about in an area represented by two square inches, especially in a complicated region, and the remaining thousand square inches of the map are merely an encumbrance; with the 2½-inch map he can move from top to bottom or from side to side of the sheet in the course of a day's trek; with the 6-inch map he may need several sheets to keep pace with his marching feet on a long straightforward walk such as the High Street range.   There's a satisfaction, hard to define because it is really more of a nuisance, in walking off the edge of one map and on to another. Have you ever tried to draw a map?   For all but the expert map-makers, this means, of course, copying an

Derwentwater

existing map.   There is nothing like it for sheer fascination and concentration.   An insignificant mistake can, and will, throw everything else wrong.   Like putting a piece in the wrong place in a jig-saw puzzle.   I love drawing maps.   Of Lakeland especially, because I love Lakeland.   I like to follow streams up from the valley to their source in the marshes of the upland combes beneath the summit crags, and if I cannot do it on the ground I like to do it on maps, my own maps. I like to stand on a summit and see the valley below as on a map.   Maps have always been my favourite literature.   I would always rather study a map than read a book, even a map of a place I have never been to and never will. Sometimes I think I should have taken up cartography as a career. But then sometimes I think I should have been a landscape gardener, sometimes a forester. Instead of which, I turn out to be an accountant, sitting in an office all day, working with figures that pass in and out of the mind. The figures that stay there permanently are Bowfell 2960, Pillar 2927, Scafell Pike 3210, and so on.

The Ordnance Survey maps are the official maps, and the best of all, but they have always had the defect of being

Patterdale

not quite reliable in the matter of footpaths on the fells. This matters little to an experienced walker, who prefers after his first few seasons to find his own way across high country (thereby savouring the real joy of fellwalking) and depends less on his map. But to a newcomer the beaten tracks are of vital concern: in bad weather they are often the only tenuous links with the safety of the valleys, the life-lines, and confidence is lost when a path is lost. Until recently, the defect was a defect of omission: many well-blazed paths found no place on the map. I remember my first visit to Helvellyn: it was a bad morning of steady rain and mist, and not really fit to leave Patterdale. But visitors to Lakeland are incorrigible optimists. They have to be. They always think the weather will improve, even though events prove them wrong time after time. The people you find huddled round a summit cairn are all optimists. Pessimists never reach the top of anything. Well, on this day the weather went from bad to worse, and the critical moment when one decides to go on because one cannot get any wetter arrived long before the gap in the wall was reached; you know which gap I mean. The mist was now thick and unmoving. The black tower at the end of Striding Edge gradually formed out of the gloom, an intimidating sight, but the Edge itself in such conditions was a magical and mysterious place, and in due course the top of Helvellyn was reached. The destination was Thirlspot, and there was no hesitation in following a wide stony path that obviously headed in that direction. According to the map, this should have led over Lower Man and White Side before turning down to the valley. But it didn't and I was mightily puzzled when it continued easily downwards into the mist, then steeply and stonily but still as wide as a road, until the gradient eased along a grassy shelf that brought me down, and out of the mist, directly above Thirlspot. A bulls-eye was scored that couldn't be missed with such a clear path underfoot. But I knew it had not taken me along the route indicated on the map. There had been no rise to Lower Man and no rise to White Side. I had used the White Stones track, even in those days a popular way up and off Helvellyn, but the Ordnance Survey did not recognise it until their post-war revisions. Their own route, more accommodating for the ponies it was originally designed for, was not a mistake of cartography but had been discarded around the turn of the century and in parts had become indiscernible on the ground. At the time I was puzzled and continued to be until a second visit in the following year, in better conditions, cleared up the mystery. There were other examples of good tracks in common use escaping the attention of the Ordnance Survey, and in later years I was stopped times without number on the fells by walkers scratching their heads over their maps and wondering where on earth they were: the path beneath their feet was obviously much-trodden, but where was it on the map? The answer was, it wasn't. Now, in their most recent editions, the Ordnance Survey have gone to the other and even more mystifying extreme: true, they have filled in many of the blanks but also filled in imaginary blanks by indicating many paths that do not exist, never have and never will. In the matter of fell paths, an error of commission is worse than one of omission. It is better for the peace of mind to find a path not shown on the map than to

waste time and temper and be assailed by doubts looking for one indicated on the map that does not exist. The omissions can be forgiven, for paths come into being quickly and the visits of the surveyors can only be infrequent, but it does seem that the latest editions have anticipated the forming of future paths along certain routes. What can be said of them, however, is that the routes wrongly indicated as visible paths are practicable and free

from hazard. Footpaths on the fells are of first importance: they show the way and avoid dangers. Panic turns to confidence when a friendly line of cairns is sighted, when the stones underfoot are scratched white by the tread of many boots, and, on occasion, one is even thankful to see a trail of litter indicating the regular passage of visitors. So footpaths became a personal study, too. If the Ordnance Survey couldn't get them right, I thought I could. I noted all I could find.

The words 'paths' and 'tracks' are almost always used without discrimination, even, as I do, to avoid repetition of the same word. But there is a difference, and it should at least be known. Paths are made, tracks are trodden. Paths are planned, tracks just happen. The best examples of paths are the former pony routes and drove roads and miners' and quarrymen's ways: you can often see the rough culverts, the retaining walls that keep the footing in place across a steep slope, the skilful use of contours. Paths are surveyed and engineered with tools. Tracks are made by boots and favour the short cut, the direct course. Paths are seldom made nowadays. The

The upper Troutbeck Valley

newer walkers' ways are tracks.   And the best tracks, which would be more properly described as paths, are those made by sheep.   The tracing of sheep-tracks on a fellside is a separate study.   I have long thought I would like to plot on a large-scale map the sheep-tracks on a fell, any fell taken at random.   But take the Kentmere slope of Harter Fell as an example.   This is scarred from top to bottom by the gravelly ravine of Drygrove Gill.   If you go up the fell by following the gill you will count scores of distinct tracks crossing from one side to the other, from one grazing ground to another, with only a few feet in altitude between one and the next.   They are perfect tracks, but a shade too narrow for the comfort of humans.   They are, in any case, rarely of much use to walkers, whose usual progression is up or down, not across.   A sheep-track may traverse the whole width of a mountain without gaining or losing more than a few feet in height.   Sheep do not like going up or down, and since their function is not to climb mountains but to eat grass they show good sense by performing it with as little effort as possible.   It is often amusing to see how boulders and other obstacles to horizontal progress are circumvented, and how persistently the same contour is maintained in the crossing of a deeply-cut beck.   Their tracks are centuries old: small dainty feet have pattered along them since long before human walkers came upon the scene.   Today we see the principles of the sheep-tracks adopted in the construction of motorways.   Our skilled engineers are learning the lessons the stupid sheep have always known.   The sheep-tracks are the oldest highways on the hills, and the best.   Sheep are neat, delicate, gentle, in all things. If you didn't know that, their footways on the mountains would tell you so.

These, then were the things—a love of the fells, a desire to escape from the common round, a longstanding interest in maps and an

Bowfell

acquired interest in drawing, an insatiable urge to look round the next corner on a trodden way if I could find one and it didn't matter if I couldn't—that caused me in the evening of November 9th 1952 to pen my first page in what I intended to be a series of seven guidebooks to the Lakeland fells, each covering a defined area, and, if you are interested, the first page I did depicted the ascent of Dove Crag from Ambleside.   I forgot to mention that I have patience.   I knew the work would take all my spare time for the next thirteen years, but it was a prospect I smacked my lips over.   Somebody once said (it would be a Chinaman, of course) that a journey of a thousand miles starts with the first step.   November 9th 1952 saw my first step.   It was a good evening for me.   It was a winter's night, but I spent it going up Dove Crag and was lost to all else.   And the nights that followed were equally good.   At that time I had no thought of publication.   I was working for my own pleasure and enjoying it hugely.   I was gathering together all my notes and drawings and a host of recollections, and putting them in a book so that when I became an old man I could look through them at leisure, recall all my memories, and go on fellwalking in spirit long after my legs had given up.   One thing worried me, however, this being the writing of the notes accompanying the illustrations.   I had adopted a bastard style of hand-printing in an attempt to produce the same legibility as metal type set by machine, but I didn't take the trouble, and it really is trouble, to get alignment at the right-hand side.   It was easy enough to start at the left-hand side, where it was necessary only to start under the start of the line above, but it was deuced hard to finish a line exactly under the finish of the last word of the line above, and I didn't make the task any easier by deciding I wouldn't break a word with a hyphen at the end of a line.   Did these things matter?   Not really, I suppose, but the pages looked untidy with the end of the lines staggered, and this began to annoy me.   So much so that in July of the following year I scrapped the hundred pages I had then done and started to do them again more meticulously, practising my wording until the lines fitted, or as nearly as I could make them.   I never quite succeeded, but the pages looked better then, neater and tidier.   They must have done because some readers have not yet realised that the finished books are not printed in the usual way.   The contrary is true.   Not a single letter of printer's type has ever appeared in any of them.   Subsequently, when it was decided to publish, I was a bit insistent about this.   I didn't want a printer interfering with my lay-outs and arrangements.   I wanted every page to be exactly as I penned it. I did everything by hand so that each page could be photographed and reproduced exactly. Another consideration was cost. It was cheaper to do it this way. This brings me to the financial aspect of the venture, about which many aspiring guide-book writers have addressed anxious questions to me, and since the story has already appeared in print, through what I regard as a breach of confidence, I may as well repeat it. By the time Book One was finished I had begun to feel that other walkers also suffering from, or rejoicing in, Lakeland fell fever, might find some use for it. Perhaps I could be an accountant and an author too. I had become quite fond of my little infant, but it was a poor frail thing and I daren't risk exposing it to the mercies of a publisher. I couldn't face the probability of rejection. That would have hurt, and anyway publishers aren't fellwalkers and wouldn't understand. What did they know of Sharp Edge who sat at a London desk? What did they know of mountain silence who lived in a world of tumult? So I took it to Sandy Hewitson, a local printer. Sandy wasn't a fellwalker either, in fact with only one leg he couldn't be, but he was a better man than most

The Stonethwaite Valley

with two: and he was a craftsman who saw in the job a challenge to his ability. I asked him how much it would cost to make copies. He said, how many copies? I thought I could reasonably expect to sell 500—you can always find 500 people ready to try anything once. Costs were worked out. 500 was clearly uneconomical. It had to be 2000 to bring the unit cost down sufficiently to permit a reasonable selling price. I asked how much 2000 would cost. Sandy said £950. I said I had only £35. He said never mind, pay me when you sell them. I did, but it took me two years, during which he never once reminded me of the debt. Sandy is dead now. He was kind to me. Kind men leave a gap when they pass on. The other sort are never missed.

Well, I needn't have worried. Books Two, Three, Four, Five, Six and Seven followed in the next eleven years. All my leisure time had been devoted to them, while gradually the garden developed into an uncharted jungle where the cats of the neighbourhood stalked their prey. There was never a single free evening when I didn't apply myself to the task with the eagerness of a lover: it was a passionate courtship. I am one of the fortunate men who bungle every household job and so am never asked to tackle anything. Between finishing one book and starting the next I paused only to refill my pipe.

Sour Milk Gill, Easedale

I was helped at first by Henry Marshall, the Kendal Librarian, who attended to the distribution and despatch of the books. He advised me that it would never do for my name to appear both as author and publisher—a sure indication that no recognised publisher could be persuaded to undertake the responsibility—and so I borrowed his name,

Blencathra, from Thirlmere

which, in any case, had more dignity than mine.   I especially liked the Henry.   I never disclosed what the Christian A of mine stood for.   It suited me to hide the truth of this affliction.   But it isn't Aloysius, if that's what you're thinking.   Subsequently this arrangement collapsed through weight of numbers.   I was having to keep records and do the invoicing and collection as well as write the books, and it was a blessed relief when the Westmorland Gazette offered to take over publication in 1963.   Henry, too, has passed on, and lies in the little churchyard in Kentmere, amongst the hills.

I was always careful to say that the series would be completed 'all being well', thus insuring myself against any conceivable mishap that might have interrupted the work.   I didn't anticipate a loss of interest or enthusiasm: I knew this couldn't happen.   What I had in mind was illness, accident, death.   Failing eyesight or a tremble in the right hand were also possibilities I feared.   Again, I needn't have worried.   The precaution was proved unnecessary.   I didn't really expect an illness.   I have never been ill, never missed a minute at work because of sickness during what is now forty-six years service.   I have reached an age when my non-walking, car-owning contemporaries are dropping like flies, but remain immune myself from any ailment, and this may be no coincidence.   Walking is almost the only exercise that a man can indulge without loss of facility from childhood to the grave.   It is a natural function of the body to walk, it isn't to drive a car . . . Nor had I any intention of having an accident. And obviously I have never died.

Seat Sandal

Accidents on the fells should never happen to walkers.   They do happen, though, but only as the result of clumsiness or a lack of ordinary common sense, never from circumstances beyond their control. It amuses me to see all the articles and treatises and even books written on the subject of walking on the fells.   Goodness me, if a person needs a manual of instruction on walking he should stay at home.   Walking is one of the first things we learn.   Our mothers taught us, remember?   We do it all our lives.   In a city street it's a matter of staying balanced on the feet while moving forward, just as we were taught as children.   On a fell it's a matter of staying balanced on the feet while moving forward, just as we were taught as children.   What else is there to learn?   Nothing.   But, unfortunately, fellwalking accidents are good news for the papers.   Sprain an ankle on Esk Hause and be helped down, and you are headlines.   Sprain an ankle in Market Street and be helped home, and who cares?   Fellwalking is not a dangerous sport.   It is not a sport at all.   It is a pleasure.   If you don't find it a pleasure, don't bother to do it and don't expect to make it a pleasure by reading a textbook.   Those who utter grave warnings about it annoy me: they are doing a disservice.   Fellwalking isn't dicing with death: it is a glorious enjoyment of life.

Fellwalking accidents happen only to those who walk clumsily.   The only advice you need (and this shouldn't be necessary either) is to watch where you are putting your feet.   Do this (and you shouldn't have to be told to do it), and you will not have an accident.   In fact, fellwalking brings immunity against accidents.   It is a wonderful exercise, the best of all.   It strengthens the legs, clears the mind, and tones up the whole body to a state of exhilaration.   You can't get these benefits through the Welfare State, nor from a doctor, nor from pills. Especially it strengthens the ankles.   Essentially, fellwalking means rough walking.   Unlike road walking, where the feet are put down in exactly the same fashion for mile after mile, on the fells the feet are rarely put down exactly the same for two steps together.   There are stony paths and bare rock, boulders and bogs, smooth grass and tussocky clumps, streams and peathags, all to be negotiated in the course of a mountain walk, and rarely is one step like the next.   All the muscles in the foot, ankle and leg are continuously exercised, not monotonously as in a road walk but in refreshing variety.   The last things to tire on rough terrain are the feet, the first things on a tarmac road are the feet.   Almost all accidents occur in descent, not in ascent.   They should never happen in descent, either.   They don't with experience.   But the novice usually expects danger in going uphill, perhaps because mountain climbing is associated with moving upwards, but you can't go up without coming down: it's half and half, and it is wrong to think that the risk of accident is over when the top is reached; it isn't, it's only just starting.   The secret, and it isn't really a secret at all because it becomes second nature with a little experience, is to keep the feet horizontal or even pointing slightly upwards when descending, and don't point them down the slope; keeping them horizontal means taking advantage of protruding stones and tufts of grass and flat ledges, and after a season or two one does this instinctively and automatically, without thinking.   Every step downwards should be planned to act as a brake.   The eye is a stride ahead of the foot all the time.   Watch where you are putting your feet, every step.   Come down the Breast Route on Great Gable with the feet horizontal and you will not slip; come down with the feet pointing down the slope and much of the journey will be done sliding on your back.   And always stop if you want to look at the view.   Don't think you can come down the Breast Route and admire the Scafells simultaneously.   For the third time, watch where you are putting your feet.

As for common sense: well, some people haven't the sense they were born with.   There is no hope for such and they should not go on the hills at all.   They invite a broken leg by jumping from boulder to boulder; they expect providence to deliver them safely if they step over the edge of a cliff, whereas providence is simply fed up with them, and won't; they wander like lost souls in mist and get into places where they can neither proceed further nor turn back, not thinking, as anyone with ordinary sense would, to leave an easy line of retreat behind them.   You can't learn common sense from a book, either.

People who go for a walk on the fells are often strongly advised to leave details of the route they intend to follow.   The idea, presumably, is that when they break their several legs the lads from Keswick and Langdale and Coniston and other places who form the rescue teams will know where to go to look for them.   Again, this miserable and misleading association of fellwalking and accidents!   Would these advisers exempt Pearson Dalton, the lone shepherd of Skiddaw House?   Poor Pearson must do his daily rounds but has nobody to tell where he is going, and only goes home at weekends: he little realises his life is in jeopardy every time he sets out! The advice may be all right for youngsters, but it is tyranny for an experienced walker to have to tell anyone where he is going if he doesn't want to.   The whole essence of fellwalking, and for this we should thank the landowners and the tenant farmers and the National Trust, is freedom to wander on the fells, and freedom to plan a route as you go along, and freedom to change your mind.   The hills are not death-traps, but invigorating playgrounds, places for exercise and the study of geology and botany and wild life.   You don't go on the hills to break your neck.   You go on the hills to get away from places where other people can break your neck.   When you step off the tarmacadam on to the rough ground, danger is past, not just beginning.   If a man arrives at Sty Head

Great Langdale

and likes the look of the Corridor Route more than the Breast Route up Great Gable, he ought to take the Corridor Route and not have it on his conscience that he told the old johnny with the bald head over the breakfast table that he would be doing Great Gable from Sty Head that day.   If, when he arrives at Sty Head, the cool waters of the tarn appeal more as the day's ultimate objective than the dusty screes of Great Gable, he ought not to feel he is not playing the game as he swims around in the sunshine: he is.   If, when he arrives at Sty Head, the weather has improved so much that he wishes to change his plans completely and traverse the Glaramara ridge instead, he ought to be able to do so with no doubts in his mind.   All he needs in his mind is to remember to watch where he is putting his feet and to use his common sense.   Too many alarms are being sounded by too many advisers.

Goat Scar, Longsleddale

Solitary fellwalking is often roundly condemned, not by solitary fellwalkers but by non-solitary fellwalkers and non-fellwalkers including coroners.   Always walk with others, they say.   This is excellent advice for those who lack ordinary gumption, or are plain daft; and such people, if they go on the fells at all, which they shouldn't, can be further advised to get themselves in the middle of a big party and keep themselves hemmed in by the sweating flesh of others.   At the end of the day they won't know where they've been and they won't have seen much, but at any rate they won't have been lost or killed themselves: they'll be proud of this, and it is not for us to reason why.   It is good advice also for those who are new to the hills until they get the feel of the high places.   But to a careful and experienced fellwalker the advice is intolerable.   It is the man or woman who walks alone who enjoys the greatest rewards, who sees and feels and senses the mood of the hills and knows them most intimately, and it is no coincidence that they are people of abundant common sense and initiative and imagination.   To the man in a conducted party the mountains are prose, to the man travelling alone they are poetry.   Of course he has nobody to talk to, which is an advantage, and there is nobody to talk to him, which is a bigger advantage; he has nothing to distract his attention and nobody to consult or argue with, he goes where he pleases, makes his own pace, halts when and where he likes, responds to nature's demands on the spot without redfaced apologies.   Absolute freedom includes freedom from the presence of others.   Some people (in parties) pity the solitary walker, and seem unable to understand that he walks alone by preference.   But surely a man doesn't have to be queer to enjoy his own company best, once in a while; away from the hills he has precious few opportunities for quiet meditation.   And if a man cannot enjoy his own company, what effect does he think it has on others?   Sometimes the reverse is the case: I always consider myself, when alone, a vastly entertaining companion, but when with others am considered unsociable, boorish, not with it.   Again, some people (in parties) confuse aloneness with loneliness, but there is all the difference in the world between being alone and being lonely.   I am least lonely when I am alone on the hills and free to indulge my imagination; most lonely in a crowd.   The worst experience that befalls a solitary walker is coming face to face with a large party, especially when they are strung out along his path. In a tight place, where this many-headed and many-legged caterpillar cannot be bypassed, it must be confronted. It may be a party of 36.   Every one of them ventures a greeting of sorts (the courtesy code of the hills, y'know). If I am in sociable mood I mumble a response to the first.   The rest must share it.   I am not going to say good-afternoon 36 times in quick succession.   The tail-end think me a surly beggar.   Okay, so I do not like large parties on the hills.   They spoil the paths.   They leave litter.   They get under the feet.   Half of them always seem to be on the point of dropping dead.   Many are obviously not enjoying themselves, and should not be there at all.   Leave the hills to those who most appreciate them is my motto.

The Screes, Wastwater

Fleetwith Pike

The Gables,
from
Great End

Langdale Pikes,
from
Great End

The Scafells, from Bowfell

Bowfell and *Langdale Pikes*

left: The approach to Scafell Pike from Esk Hause

above: The approach to Crinkle Crags from Three Tarns

Helvellyn, from Fairfield

right: Haystacks and Scarth Gap, from Gamlin End

Sad Gill, Longsleddale

Mickledore and Scafell Crag

Haystacks

Wasdale Head Church

Brothers Water

I mentioned mist. Nothing is more terrifying to the uninitiated. In their minds, tormented by grim warnings, mist is associated with getting lost, with walking in circles, with fatal accidents. It is true that one tends to walk in circles, clockwise, in country that lacks distinctive features. I remember once walking up the path from Wrynose Pass to Red Tarn and leaving it to make the short, untracked beeline to the top of Cold Pike: the ground at first is fairly flat, with grassy swells. Everything was hidden in mist. After twenty minutes I found myself on a good path, which I knew shouldn't be there. It was the path I had left, a hundred yards further on. I set off again in the right direction but after a further twenty minutes found myself back on the same path once more, after which I abandoned Cold Pike and let the path take me down into Langdale. Walking in circles is amusing and interesting, but not frightening. Getting lost shouldn't happen. There are two kinds of mist on the hills, never fog. There is dry mist, which floats around the fellsides like a gossamer veil, always mobile but clinging to the gullies and hollows: it drifts silently across the scene, one moment impenetrable, the next torn into windows that give exquisite glimpses of the far distance in a white surround, the next vanished completely. Of all weather conditions on the fells, the most fascinating is dry mist. There is no venom in it, only a playful mischief. More than anything, mist expresses the atmosphere of the mountains. Mountains generate mist and look naked without their delicate white shawls. The effects are often startling, often incredibly beautiful, always interesting, never frightening. But the other sort of mist is wet mist, hanging immovably over the tops, its lower limit a horizontal line as straight as though drawn with a ruler. This is cloud, charged with raindrops,

High Sweden Bridge, Scandale

and causing saturation as surely as a torrential downpour; there is no pleasure in such conditions, and those who walk for pleasure, as all should, give the tops a miss on such days. Mist is never so thick that one cannot see one's hands in front of one's face, and those who claim to have experienced mist like this are telling fibs. In the thickest mist or cloud visibility is never down to less than ten yards in the hours of daylight, enough to follow a beaten track, and it is to defeat these conditions that the lines of cairns have been erected to indicate the most frequented routes. Then the cairns become friendly guides and many a lost soul has had occasion to bless them with the fervour of a Tibetan pilgrim reaching a prayer-shrine. Dry mist is a charmer, wet mist a snare, but neither is the cause of accidents. Clumsy walking is the cause of accidents. If clumsy walkers did no more than damage themselves they would be welcome to go on doing it, but they also spoil the paths for everybody else. Bulls in china shops are gentle creatures compared with some of the pedestrians one sees, and hears, in Rossett Gill or Little Hell Gate or Lord's Rake. They are often verbally noisy, a common characteristic of the inefficient, but it is their boots that cause most clatter. Flying stones, uprooted sods, and blasphemous shouts accompany their

*Pike o' Stickle, from **Blea Tarn***

sliding progress, especially downhill, in a surround of noise. At home, one imagines, there will not be a cup with a handle, not a chair without broken springs, not a door with a knob left on. But a good walker moves silently and is a joy to behold. He moves not gracefully, but rhythmically. His footstep is firm. He presses the path into place with his boots, and improves it. The clumsy walker loosens and destroys paths. A good walker loves the zigzags of a path, which always give the easiest progression, but a bad walker can't be bothered, cuts across them and ruins them for others. A good walker always gives the impression of moving leisurely, even slowly, and having time to spare; a bad walker always seems to be in a hurry. A good walker will climb Scafell Pike from Sty Head and hardly disturb a single stone; a bad walker will leave a trail of debris. Their respective journeys through life will be the same.

I have mentioned boots, and might borrow Kipling's song title to emphasise the word thrice, because boots are the best footgear for the hills. But wear shoes or sandals or go barefoot if any of these suit you better. Reams have been written on what to wear on the hills, but ignore such advice. The thing is to wear what is most comfortable. It is a matter of individual choice; don't be dictated to. Clothes never become comfortable until they are shabby and shapeless and well perforated by sparks from the pipe; at least, mine don't, and when you can no longer appear at the office in them without shame they are ready to serve you on the hills, where nobody is there to see them and wouldn't bother if they did. Comfort is the thing. Comfort includes keeping warm and dry, but ways of achieving it differ widely. The most ghastly apparitions appear on the fells, spectral creatures and scarecrows on two legs, representing varying conceptions of the ideal mountain garb. If sheep didn't have such good manners they would laugh their heads off. Clothing is an individual matter. You don't have to look like the man in front. As with everything else, one learns from experience.

A lot of advice has been given by various authorities on equipment: the need for taking a map and compass and a whistle (they never mention guide books, drat them!), on stoves and cooking gear, on exposure meters and lenses and filters and so on. And a lot of rot has been said. Well, please yourself if you want to carry a load of hardware and ironmongery around, but don't make fellwalking a game to be played by rules. It is a pleasure, as I have said, or it is not fellwalking at all; it is something to enjoy or something to endure: it cannot be both. You see hikers setting forth for a day on the hills burdened as though they were starting a six-months expedition to Antarctica: they are grim and anguished of face when they ought to be carefree and smiling. They are not going into uncharted wastes and should have no more sense of apprehension or impending risk than if they were going for a Sunday afternoon stroll in the park. The hills are friendly: there are no lurking hazards, no

Packhorse Bridge, Wasdale Head

traps around every corner.   The dangers have been absurdly exaggerated; there are too many gloomy prophets around, and too many people ready with advice, including me.   You are not making a date with death.   You are not making a technical excursion into space.   You are going for a walk, that's all, no different from all other walks except that there is more up and down and the way is likely to be rougher, and you are going to see and enjoy beautiful scenery, wild and lonely places and visions of loveliness that will bring tears to your eyes and joy to your heart at the same time; but you are far more likely to run into danger crossing the main street of Keswick. If you get into trouble on the fells it will be your own fault; in the main street of Keswick it might not be.   The fells are not monsters, but amiable giants.   You can romp over them and pull the hairs on their chests and shout in their ears and treat them rough, and they don't mind a bit.   They are not enemies to be wrestled with.   They are friends.   Go amongst them as you go amongst friends.

For me, a map and a camera are enough: the map to look at now and then and to study if I have to spend an hour under a boulder out of the rain, that is, for company; and the camera for recording permanently the transient, often fleeting, beauty of a landscape caressed by sun and shadow.   I have never carried a compass, preferring to rely on a good sense of direction, and in my case the latter has always proved reliable, more than a compass could ever be and certainly less fiddling to consult.   But all authorities insist that a compass should be taken. so perhaps you should.   In my

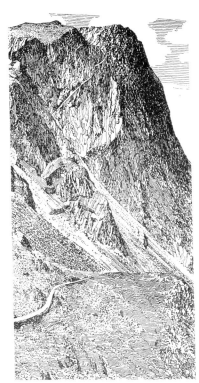

Honister Crag

case, I don't because I have never bothered to understand how a compass works or what it is supposed to do. To me a compass is a gadget, and I don't get on well with gadgets, of any sort. They never seem to work for me as they do for other people. My mind is full of dreams and imaginings and romance, and is strictly non-technical. The fells are honest and have no gadgets. Anything operated by a mechanism is away over my head. Wheels and switches and levers and things belong to another world, not mine. I have tried hard to understand, heaven knows. I have studied simple mechanisms intently for hours. But they will not work for me. I could never solve bent-nail puzzles or unravel knots. You cannot appreciate the awful and utter loneliness of a man who does not understand gadgets in a world that is becoming full of them, and in a life that cannot be lived without them. People who ask me why I haven't a motor car are turning a knife in my heart. But I have found that there is always somebody who knows and is ready to come to the rescue, somebody who will pityingly and patronisingly offer to do it for me. In fact, it's not at all bad not being able to do things. Other people do them for you, not really out of kindness but because they like to demonstrate their superior intellect. You get your knots unravelled: you get jobs done for you. You get free rides in motor cars, and admire the passing

Harrison Stickle, from Blea Tarn

scenery while other people drive and get their hands dirty and pay the petrol bills. You remain an innocent in these matters. Cameras have gadgets, of course. Mine is a second-hand one, a simple one with various contrivances such as range-finder, flash-bulb and self-portrait device, but I don't know which is which or what they are supposed to do, and leave them alone. I can put a new film in and take a used one out, and know which knob to press to take a picture (my baby son showed me) but the rest is a closed book I have never been able to open. I have the same trouble with gates. Gates are gadgets to close an opening in a wall or fence. Hundreds of them are encountered in the intakes and on the lower slopes, but there seems to be as many ways of fastening a gate as there are gates. No two are quite alike. With some of them you can't tell which end is supposed to open. A good tip is first to determine which end has the hinges: in theory, it is the other end that opens, or should. My heart drops when I see them across my path. They mean confusion and delay. I spend hours every year trying to open gates. A few are obvious and simple, but many are too ingenious for me. Some can't be made to open at all. Then they have to be climbed, and nine times out of ten the same thing happens. You get one foot on the bottom rung, which stays firm until your other leg is at its maximum height when being thrown over the other side, whereupon it collapses and so do you upon the top rung, cruelly impaling delicate organs of the body thereon. My, how it hurts! Sometimes the pain creases you for the rest of the day. Perhaps I should have recounted this latter experience in the first person, not knowing how women fare when bisected in this fashion. In fact, I suffered quite a bit during the making of those guidebooks. But never as the result of a walking accident. I always watch where I am putting my feet. It's the man-made gadgets that defeat and destroy me. Talking of cameras reminds me that I have not yet stated the real excuse for writing this book. It's the photographs. Here I must be modest as befits my amateur status with a camera. I don't profess to know much about lenses and shutters and related contrivances, and never had, or wanted, an exposure meter, which always sounds to me rather indecent. I have an eye for a good subject, but trust to luck in capturing it. I get the oddest results. Some pictures that should be absolute winners turn out to be grey and drab and worthless; some despairing snaps turn out better than expected. I must have taken thousands of pictures on my walks. Most were adequate for my purpose, to record some detail, but just occasionally,

Wasdale Head

and often enough by mischance, there is a good one in the batch from the chemist's. Out of thousands, some are bound to be up to standard. The photographs in this book are my best, and they are the real justification for the book. The rest is padding. I'm just filling in the middle pages with this narrative.

I had the title for this book, FELLWANDERER, before the contents. I liked it, although it suggested an autobiography, which is the next to the last thing I would ever dream of doing. FELLWANDERING would perhaps overcome this difficulty, but in turn suggested a manual of walking instruction, which is positively the last thing I would ever dream of doing, believing such a book to be quite unnecessary except for half-wits. The readers of my guidebooks are not half-wits. They are people of exceptional charm and intelligence and enthusiasm for the fells. Not the least of my rewards has been a constant stream of appreciative letters from all manner of folk and from all sorts of unlikely places. Some were straightforward enquiries about accommodation and itineraries and mountain campsites and the like, and some simply recounted personal experiences and adventures.   But a thousand I have kept, and I count them a thousand treasures.   People have been very kind, and many letters have been quite touching, the sort that humble a man and shame his conceit. Some were from lame or infirm people, who had found a few of the easier climbs within their powers and wrote to express their joy for experiences they thought they could never share with the more fortunate.   Some were from people in hospital beds, who had wondered what the mountains of Lakeland were really like, and now felt they knew; some were from people beset by worry and anxiety who had turned to the hills for the first time and there found the solace they needed, and had since become regular visitors; some were from elderly people who had long looked at the fells but never dared to venture upon them until they were given confidence; some were from servicemen in far-off countries who yearned for the hills of their homeland; some were from exiles born in the shadow of the fells who had never forgotten or ceased to love them; some contained generous offers of hospitality in the remoter districts, or the use of cars and services as chauffeurs.   Many were from fathers and mothers who had been encouraged to take their children on the tops and by doing so had transformed their family life and forged new bonds between themselves.   And many, a great many, were from the children themselves, telling of their wonderful adventures in simple words that are often the most effective.   Do take the children on the hills early, in a rucksack on your shoulders if they can't yet walk.   Children are born scramblers and don't hurt easily: it's yourself you want to watch, not them.   They will be in a seventh heaven of delight.   They don't fear the elements or the mountains or monstrous apparitions in gas capes.   Fear only comes with age. It always pleases me to see a family party on a mountain track.   There, I think, goes a good father and an even better mother.   They have the right idea.   They want their children to know and love the quiet places before the noisy world offers less desirable outlets for juvenile enthusiasm and energy and enterprise.   A child forgets many incidents of childhood, but he will always remember the day his old dad took him along the Climbers Traverse on Bowfell and up the Great Slab.   There are red-letter days in infancy, too.

Yes, all my correspondents were kind.   I tried to acknowledge all letters, but could do so only briefly, and too often after unseemly delay.   I used to build up a cairn of unanswered letters on my desk, and still do, and when it collapsed reply to a few and build up the rest again. There really hasn't been time to give them the attention they deserved, and I'm sorry. People have told me their difficulties and troubles, too, but never once in a complaining fashion, and I have marvelled at their fortitude and resolve. You know, we who are fit and well and able to enjoy life fully ought to count our blessings more. We are the fortunate ones. It makes for humility to read of others counting their blessings who have far less to count. Those of us who have most cause to do it, rarely trouble. We take things for granted far too much these days. We who have the best reason to be satisfied are often the least satisfied. We grab for more when we have enough already.

Writers of guidebooks always strive to get their facts right, knowing there will be reprimands if they don't. I have often travelled a hundred miles merely to check the existence or position of a particular wall or sheepfold, or to verify a small detail that was not clear in my mind, or to be absolutely sure that a certain mountain can be seen from a certain other. But the way of the perfectionist is hard. Facts don't stay right. The letters come in. "Dear Mr. Wainwright, you omitted to indicate a stile . . ." I didn't. It's been put up since. "Why didn't you show this path? . . ." Because there wasn't any path when I was there in 1956. "You showed a signpost and there isn't one . . ." You're dead right, mate, somebody took it for firewood. In Book Seven, not yet published as I write this, I draw particular attention to the new stretcher-box on Shamrock Traverse, describing it as a useful landmark to guide walkers across a rough section of country. In this

Summit cairn, Great End

morning's paper I read with dismay that the box had disintegrated because of frost, and unless the Cockermouth Rescue Team rescue my reputation by replacing it I shall have more puzzled correspondents to pacify. Guidebooks are quickly out of date, some even, as in this instance, before they leave the printers.   Some facts stay right.   Seven times four is always twenty-eight.   I would have enjoyed a greater peace of mind if I had published a book of multiplication tables.   Or would I?   On reflection, no, I wouldn't, of course not.   Peace of mind comes to me on the hills.   The changes that take place are trivial, merely a plucking of little threads in the tremendous backcloth of the mountain scene, and of no consequence in the general pattern.   Mickledore will be just the same in a thousand years, Sharp Edge no less sharp, Sty Head no less exciting.   The hills will always be there, always giving peace of mind.

   Some readers have helped me by drawing my attention to certain features they thought worth mentioning.   Molly Lefebure was one who did her best to help.   She tried.   She told me of a stone circle she had discovered on Burnbank Fell during a fox-hunt.   I must not mention the circumstances that led to its discovery, but I kept the antiquity in mind as 'Molly's Shame' until I visited the area.   But could I, in due course, find a stone circle on Burnbank Fell?   No, I couldn't.   I spent a month of Saturdays crawling around Burnbank Fell almost on hands and knees in a vain search for it, at first eagerly, but latterly as a man without hope.   'Molly's Shame' became 'Molly's Folly'.   I climbed walls and fences, not heeding discomfort, as though seeking the Holy Grail. The reward—nothing.   The cost—a great hole torn in my pants by barbed wire, and in such a vital place that I had to partake of tea at a Loweswater hotel with legs tightly crossed, and wear my plastic mac all the way home although the day was sunny and warm.   I gave up after that.   I wrote to the lady, gently: "There is NO stone circle on Burnbank Fell, love.   The village lads must have been larking about."   Stung to the quick, she set out to prove me wrong.   Let me quote from her next letter: "Well, to tell you the ghastly truth, I have made one or two little sorties there myself recently; and found, nothing.   But you must believe that I did originally find a circle; and as proof of my perfect conviction of this circle let me tell you that I, when I first went back, proceeded straight to where I believed this circle to be: I went straight to it like a wretched homing pigeon. I was alone, but if I had had you or anyone else with me such a companion would have noticed how I went to

Ullswater, from St. Sunday Crag

the presumed place without a second's hesitation. It was a real blow when there was no circle! These preliminary fruitless trips unsettled me: still, it is easy to mistake a place on a fellside. Then came your cry that you were giving up the search. And that there was, or is, no circle. Well, on Tuesday I went once again to Burnbank Fell with some German friends who have been staying here and an assortment of children. This was to be the final expedition to end all expeditions, and, since I believed I would ultimately find the circle (in spite of all you said), I took a camera, a notebook, a compass, a pencil or two, and a metal measuring rod thing that flips back into a metal spool, weighs very heavy and is extremely dangerous: have your finger off in no time if you relaxed your guard for an instant. This scientific equipment was designed to record the indisputable evidence of a circle, with which evidence A.W. was going to be crushed. The search party was scientifically lined up each person taking a contour, and off we went: very slowly, inch by inch examining the ground. This went on all day, the search in final desperation being extended to Mockerkin How. We found four dead sheep, a lot of mosquitoes and an abominable species of particularly brutal thistle that gave me such a jab in the leg that I thought for one panic-stricken moment that I had been bitten by an adder, and I was about to start screaming and demanding to be rushed to hospital for snake-bite serum when fortunately I noticed the thistle. This was a blessing, for everybody was already looking at me askance because of getting them all out there in that place of desolation on such a beautiful day when we could have been by Crummock Water. An imaginary stone circle was bad enough, an imaginary snake into the bargain would have been the final final straw. The search was prolonged and resulted in nothing but the Aga being out when we got home and dinner arriving on the table, in consequence, at the hour of twenty minutes to twelve, midnight. It was a delicious dinner, and gaiety abounded, the hostess being particularly lively—but with a

The Buttermere Valley, from Brandreth

Scots Pine, Dora's Field

heavy load lurking in the secret recesses of her heart. For, to tell you the truth, I am now of the opinion myself that there is no longer a stone circle on Burnbank Fell, Mr. Wainwright darling. I cannot possibly think what can have happened to it; that I found it I have no doubt. It was there, exact and perfect and melancholy and deserted, and indeed should be known not as my Shame nor a Folly but as Molly's Magic Circle." And a bitter extract from mine, in reply: "The Franco-German sweep across the flanks of Burnbank Fell deserved the wide canvas of a Cecil B. de Mille spectacular. The march of Lefebure and her forces across those barren wastes was epic stuff, the best thing since Moses or somebody led the children of Israel across the desert. Never was an operation more carefully planned, never were troops more skilfully deployed, never was a crusade more sure of success. The battle orders were simple: search for a stone circle marked· LADIES. But as the hours passed, as the sun wheeled across the sky, as Lefebure hoarsely urged on her faltering legions throughout the long day until they were no more than black silhouettes against the darkening gloom, as, finally, the disorganised and despondent rabble, crushed to defeat and near to rebellion, trailed in disarray back o'er the hills whence they came, then the star of Wainwright shone brightly over the deserted moor."   I keep telling Molly our letters to each other (suitably edited) should be published: they would bring the house down.

I could have written a better book if I had some personal adventures to recount.   But I haven't, none worth the telling. The thirteen years have been a dreamlike procession of happy uneventful days. The minor disappointments of climbing a fell to note the view and then finding the top shrouded in mist, or having to come down prematurely to catch a bus, or getting soaked with nothing to show for it, were soon forgotten. I always got a walk anyway, and a good tea. I never had an accident, or a fall, I was never benighted in a blizzard or tossed by a bull. I always walked alone.   By

Pillar, from Great Gable

preference.   I would have been poor company, anyway.   I had work to do—maps to check, details of ascents to note, photographs to take, views to record—and could not afford distractions.   Furthermore I had this work to do unseen or at least unnoticed by others.   If there's one thing I cannot stand, it's someone looking over my shoulder.   If there's another, it's someone asking silly questions.   If there's another, it's being pointed out.   I suffer fools badly.   So I had to be anonymous, and what a furtive character I became!   It was funny really.   My general appearance was fairly well known among walkers, due to some unwelcome publicity.   My height and size I couldn't disguise.   If I discarded my spectacles I would have fallen over a cliff.   Harry Griffin had described me in one of his books as rather distinguished looking, which pleased me on the whole although I never quite forgave him the qualifying adjective.   Older readers will remember that there used to be a character known as Lobby Lud, and if you spotted him amongst the seaside crowds you were given a reward. £5, I think.   It was a newspaper stunt.   Well, I became another Lobby Lud, but I didn't hand out rewards. I knew many people were on the lookout for me: they had told me so by letter.   They knew approximately where I was operating, or at least they knew the area I was working on.   Yes, I was furtive all right.   I liked a fell to myself, and particularly a summit.   These conditions I often found, especially in the remoter and little-known districts, and here I was really happy and could work undisturbed.   On the more popular fells I had to observe many subterfuges to keep out of other people's way.   If a summit was already occupied upon arrival I had to hang about in the vicinity until it was vacated.   If others were coming along my path I wandered off it a while, behind a wall or a boulder, to avoid conversation.   I have no doubt at all that those who were bypassed thus thought I had detoured to obey a call; the same call, incidentally, I can claim to have obeyed on every square mile of Lakeland and with special satisfaction in Manchester's gathering grounds.   I was not always successful, I mean in avoiding people, and the inevitable happened on a few occasions.   I kept hearing stories of other solitary walkers who may have borne some resemblance, poor lads, who were having a rough time of it ('Mr. Wainwright, I presume?') but I did pretty well myself.   If challenged, my answer depended on the circumstances obtaining at the time and on the age and particularly the sex of the questioner.   Yes, I made the acquaintance of some nice ladies.   There was one, however, to whom I owe a profound apology, and I had better get it off my conscience now, because she will certainly read this book and recognise herself. It happened on the summit of High Stile on a glorious Sunday afternoon, 26th July 1964. She was seated by the cairn and accompanied by a small boy, having apparently come up from Buttermere. I was in a desperate hurry to catch a bus at Ennerdale Bridge, there was no time to wait for her to depart, and conditions were ideal for two photographs I needed to complete my panorama from the summit. I sat down a few yards away and got my pictures. She said, are you Mr. Wainwright? No, I said. Well, she said, I know what he looks like and you look like him and I know he's working in this area at present; I do so want to meet him. I was a bit sorry then; my chances with the ladies were few and far between, but there was that confounded bus and the cock had already crowed once. No, I said again, but I know who you mean. Then off I went, and looking back later saw her leave the summit. I'm sorry, lass, whoever you are. There were others to whom I said yes, others to whom I said no. People in parties always got a no. I adopted the name of A. Walker, which I thought very clever. The A here can stand for Aloysius, if you want.

On a few occasions I went on the fells at night, climbing up in the dusk, finding a simple promenade near the summit where I could move about slowly and safely to keep warm, for even a summer's night can be bitterly cold up aloft, and moving off with the dawn. There is no question of sleep and it is a waste of energy to carry a sleeping bag or a tent. If you are alone, the experience is eerie. On a still night the silence is absolute. There is nothing to see but the black silhouette of the nearby slopes and the skyline, and, sometimes, the moon and a million stars. The hours of darkness drag. You think. You live your life over again. You try to remember, in sequence, the names of the football teams that have won the cup in the past ten years. You try to recall all the women who might have married you if you had asked them, and this passes the time along well, not because there are so many but because there are so many doubts about the few. You ration yourself to a cigarette or a pipe every half-hour. You keep trying to kid yourself that it is getting lighter, that the dawn is breaking. Eventually it does, after what seems an Arctic winter, and it is rarely the glorious spectacle the poets tell us about: much more likely it will be grey and damp and you will find that mist has silently shrouded the top. But the experience is a profound one: it attunes you to the mountains until you feel a part of the living rock; and there is the company of the sheep, which seek out their resting places when darkness falls and, as in all other things, are dainty and silent sleepers. Once you have spent a night on a mountain you are never again awed by it but think of it with affection. The best bivouac I had was on Harrison Stickle. The evening was fine and I was in position before dark, near the headwaters of Dungeon Gill. For a time I was privileged to watch a fox on a grassy shelf below me, obviously enjoying life, playing alone like a kitten, rolling around on its back like a dog; and not for the first time I fell to wondering whether foxhunting was a cruel sport that should be stopped. Those who practise it say it isn't, that the fox has a fair chance of escape and will escape if it is clever enough, and that, if caught, the end is sudden and merciful. All this is true, but they go too far if they say that the fox actually enjoys being hunted. Only a fox knows this and no fox ever said so. It may, until the awful moment of realisation that there is not going to be any escape this time, that the enemy has won, that the snapping jaws of the hounds can no longer be avoided: there is no enjoyment then, but terror. Yet this, after all, is nature's way. The buzzard swoops on the vole, the cat on the mouse. It is better than man's way, with guns or poisons. The

Red Screes and the Troutbeck Valley

dalesmen think so, too.   I remember walking up out of Longsleddale one morning and coming across a shepherd leaning on a gate just below Wren Quarry.   He asked me whether I had seen any men with guns down in the valley.   I said I had, and then he told me that he had heard a whisper that a fox-shoot had been arranged for that day, on Harter Fell, and that he had forestalled it by going up on the fell early with his dogs and driving the foxes away over the other side of Mardale: they'll be wasting their time, he said with satisfaction.   This man told me of foxes he had seen crippled by gunshot, painfully dying a slow death because they could no longer search for food, and he himself had no doubt that hunting with hounds was the only merciful way of keeping the numbers under control.   But it's a beastly business, this slaughter of animals.   The worst crime the human race ever committed, or permitted, and it has committed and permitted plenty, was the deliberate introduction of a filthy disease to rid the world of rabbits, a slow lingering tormented death of the innocents.   I never forgave the human race for that.   There was no protest march to Aldermaston or Trafalgar Square on behalf of the rabbits; man marches in protest only to save his own skin . . .   But back to the hills.   I was telling you of my night on Harrison Stickle.   During the hours of darkness a thin drizzle set in.   An insidious wet veil was drawn across the fell and stayed until just before daylight, when it cleared.   I was glad of the opportunity to exercise my legs when a reluctant dawn lightened the sky, and climbed up to the cairn overlooking Langdale.   The scene I saw then was the most beautiful I have ever witnessed.   The tops were clear, although stark and sullen in the half-light, but below me the valley was completely filled by a white mist that extended from the steep upthrust of Rossett Pike at the dalehead and curved like an unbroken glacier, following the contours of the valley away into the distance over Elterwater and above the length of Windermere to the sea, a river of vapour, a mantle of unblemished purity.   It was enough to make a man weep.   There was complete stillness in the air and a profound silence over all.   Far below, somewhere beneath the ceiling of mist, I could hear the cocks crowing.   There were people in their beds down there who knew nothing of the glory of the morning.   I stayed until the sun rose and coloured the peaks in a soft glow.   Then there was movement, the mist gradually breaking up and revealing the patchwork of fields in the valley, and in a few minutes only a few white puffballs floated in the still air.   It was time to be off.   The   sheep had already left their couches among the boulders and were patiently and perseveringly foraging, as they would do without intermission until another dusk ended another day.   Completely contented, and having amazing fortitude, the sheep are the truest lovers of the high places.   Come rain, come wind, they are happy with little.   Unlike man, often miserable with much, they never complain.

If I spent the rest of my life telling of my memories of the fells, time would defeat me.   There are so many. Some are still vivid in the mind, some have become dreamy with the passing of years.   But all are pleasant, and many beautiful.   There have been days of drenching rain, but I have always been content to spend time in the lee of boulder or crags, watching the rise and fall of the mists. The first drop of cold water that gets through your defences and runs an erratic course down your ribs is always the worst: those that follow matter less.   You can get wet through to the skin, and yet glow with health.   There have been days of perishing cold, when I have huddled by summit cairns and made notes with hands turned blue and stiff, but five minutes walking brings back a tingling warmth.   There have been days of fierce wind, a worse enemy than rain or cold, when climbing a mountain meant fighting a battle, too: a battle that left me not weak but strong, for these tussles with the elements

Ennerdale Water, from High Stile

do a power of good, freeing the mind from worldly worries and strengthening the body. I have caught many a bad cold at the office, never a one on the hills. Snow is a more subtle adversary. It transforms the fells into fields of dazzling whiteness and the distant scene into a fairy wonderland. It is beautiful, beautiful, but treacherous. Snow is feminine, a temptress: when you meet her, watch your step. When her seduction hardens into ice, avoid her. The fells are best left alone after frost. And in thunderstorms. But it is the warm sunny days that remain most clearly etched in the memory: the beautiful days of blue skies and dappled clouds; the quiet days when rain and wind have slunk away, seemingly for ever; the lazy days when life holds no greater joy than to lie on the ground and idly listen to the music of a tumbling stream, soft music with never a discord, and watch the dramas being played by moving pinheads in the grass; there is another world of activity here and life is exciting: there are bullies and cowards and heroes, and eager lovers and swooning females. But most of all the daffodils of Ullswater haunted Wordsworth:

Fleetwith Pike, Buttermere

it is the bewitching beauty of Lakeland that haunts the mind, as scenes that pass across the inward eye as a pageant of loveliness.

Not so much the scenes preferred by the tourists—Ashness Bridge, Friar's Crag, Orrest Head—charming though they are, but the unexpected scenes, those revealed by a movement of mist, those that dramatically come into view on the last few steps to a summit cairn, those that stop a walker in his tracks as he rounds a corner and glimpses a picture beautiful beyond belief, those that occur in early morning when the sun breaks through the mist over the valley, or in the evening when one is loth to leave the peace of the tops and enjoys the reward of perfect sunsets.   Or the memories in miniature, the more intimate charm of sparkling waterfalls in ferny dells, of winter birches touched by sunlight against a dark sky, of squirrels running along a wall, of trees laden with new snow, of translucent waters in rocky pools, of lonely rowans splashing grey rocks with vivid colour, of hovering buzzards motionless in the sky and ravens in tumbling flight, of wood-smoke rising lazily from farm chimneys in the quiet of evening, of sheepdogs watching intently every movement of their masters and refusing to be distracted, of newborn lambs and their proud mothers.   Oh, a pen cannot tell of these joys.   A walk in Lakeland is a walk in heaven.

Stirrup Crag, Yewbarrow

Mountain climbing satisfies an instinct all men should feel: the urge to get to the top.   It is natural for a man to look up, to strive to attain something higher and out of his immediate reach, to overcome the difficulties and disappointments of his upward progress, to exult at his ultimate success.   Mountain climbing is an epitome of life, and good practice for it.   You start at the bottom, the weaklings and the irresolute drop out on the way up, the determined reach the top.   Life is like that.

My space is nearly finished.   I could have used it better, but the words that would more adequately tell the glory of the fells are not known to me.   Like a lover who can only keep repeating the same three words because there are no others that say more, I have found the pen, in my hands, no instrument for describing the captivating charm of Lakeland.   Lakeland is an emotion, and emotions are felt, not expressed.

I will close by wishing you many many happy days on the fells.   You will be following in my footsteps, wherever you go, and I hope you find the enjoyment I found: I am sure you will.   Please be helpful to the people you meet, and please be kind to the birds and animals.   Don't forget to watch where you are putting your feet, and you'll be all right.

Seatoller

Would I could start my fellwanderings all over again! But time is running out. Every day that passes is a day less. That day will come when there is nothing left but memories. And afterwards, a last long resting place by the side of Innominate Tarn, on Haystacks, where the water gently laps the gravelly shore and the heather blooms and Pillar and Gable keep unfailing watch. A quiet place, a lonely place. I shall go to it, for the last time, and be carried: someone who knew me in life will take me and empty me out of a little box and leave me there alone.

And if you, dear reader, should get a bit of grit in your boot as you are crossing Haystacks in the years to come, please treat it with respect. It might be me.

Sour Milk Gill, Easedale

Crummock Water

Summit of Knott Rigg, looking to Eel Crag, High Spy

Blencathra and Newlands, from Robinson

Innominate Tarn, Haystacks and Great Gable

Unnamed tarn, Haystacks and High Crag

Patterdale, looking to Kirkstone Pass

St. Sunday Crag, Grisedale and Helvellyn

Summit of Whiteless Pike, looking to Sail and Causey Pike

The Scafell group, from Grasmoor

Blencathra and Derwentwater, from Maiden Moor

Blencathra and Clough Head, from Causey Pike

The Scafells, from Wastwater

Haystacks and the High Stile range

Blea Water Crag, High Street

Hobcarton Crag, Hopegill Head

Wastwater

The Scafells, from Middle Fell

The Fairfield group and Brothers Water

The head of Longsleddale

The Buttermere Valley from Kirkstile

Skiddaw, from Baggra Yeat

Summit of Harter Fell, looking to the Scafells

The head of Eskdale

Summit of Fisher Crag, Thirlmere, looking to Blencathra

Pillar and Scoat Fell, from Ennerdale Water

Water lilies on a mountain tarn

Swirl How, from Brim Fell

Summit cairn, Lingmell

Summit of King's How, looking to Skiddaw

Borrowdale, from Thorneythwaite Fell

The Scafell group, from Hindscarth

Gatesgarth and Fleetwith Pike, from High Stile